THE
SEED
VAULT

First published in 2019
by Eyewear Publishing Ltd
Suite 333, 19-21 Crawford Street
Marylebone, London W1H 1PJ
United Kingdom

Cover design and typeset by Edwin Smet
Author photograph by Cory Harbour
Printed in England by TJ International Ltd, Padstow, Cornwall

The right of Lucas Jacob to be identified as author of
this work has been asserted in accordance with section 77
of the Copyright, Designs and Patents Act 1988
ISBN 978-1-912477-88-3

*The editor has generally followed American spelling and punctuation
at the author's request.*

WWW.EYEWEARPUBLISHING.COM

for Madison

Lucas Jacob
is the author of the chapbooks
A Hole in the Light (Anchor & Plume Press, 2015)
and *Wishes Wished Just Hard Enough* (Seven Kitchens Press, 2019).
He has received the Gival Press Tri-Language Poetry Prize and
the Houston Poetry Festival's Lucille Johnson Clark Award.
His work has appeared in journals including *Southwest Review,*
RHINO, Hopkins Review, and *Valparaiso Poetry Review*. He earned
his Bachelor's degree at Carleton College (MN) and his Master's
at Temple University (PA). For more than twenty years,
he has been a teacher and administrator in K-12 schools across
the United States. In 2004-05, he had the privilege
of serving as a Fulbright Teaching Fellow in Budapest,
Hungary. A native of the Chicago area, he now lives in
Indianapolis, Indiana. *The Seed Vault* is his first
full-length collection.

TABLE OF CONTENTS

I

SUSPENSION — 10

HUNGARIAN SONNET 1 — 11

LISTENING TO THE BLUES ON A THURSDAY MORNING — 12

RECURRENCE — 13

TREMOR — 14

AGAINST NOSTALGIA — 16

ROUTE 501 SOUTH — 17

AT DINOSAUR VALLEY, GLEN ROSE, TX — 18

SURVIVAL TIP: LIVING THROUGH THE NIGHT — 20

HOW TO TEACH THE WRITING OF POETRY — 22

2 TRAM, BUDAPEST — 23

THE CRICKETS & THE CEILING FAN — 24

GLOBE — 25

THE CURVATURE OF THE EARTH — 26

SNOWBOUND — 28

WATCHING HUMMINGBIRDS AT CEDAR CREEK LAKE, TX — 31

TOLL — 32

II

WINNER — 34

GREATNESS — 35

WALL — 36

INDUSTRY — 38

BAN — 39

FORCE — 40

DEAL — 41

CARNAGE — 42

WORK — 43

SECURITY — 44

REFUGE — 45

THREAT — 46

III

SAN ANTONIO TRIPTYCH — 48

AGAINST DESPAIR — 51

LETTING DOWN YOUR GUARD — 52

PATH OF TOTALITY — 54

FROM A MCDONNELL-DOUGLAS MD 80 — 55

A LULLABY IN MARCH — 56

PLANETARIUM — 57

BLACK MOON — 58

MORE FLIES WITH HONEY — 59

TUTORIAL — 60

PRAYING MANTIS — 61

TO THE BOY IN A LONDON LEAF-FALL… — 63

MILE STONES — 65

PUPPY LOVE — 66

UNTOUCHED — 68

THE NEXT DAY — 69

IN PRAISE OF MORTALITY — 70

IV

VAVILOV AT SARATOV — 73

NOTES — 88

ACKNOWLEDGEMENTS — 90

I

SUSPENSION

To float on your back, arms spread out wide,
fingers riding the skim of the pool's surface,
legs stretched from your hips and loose at your knees,
the sounds of all things below amplified
and all things above blunted by the filters
that are the air bubbles in each ear,
and not to kick at the pavement that is not
supporting your feet or to twist at the neck
to measure the distance to contact,
is to have faith that the water will hold you,
and this in turn is the faith that the trees
whose leaves leap back into focus at each
opening of your eyes will not fall,
and this the faith that the sun that reddens
the insides of your eyelids will not go out,
and that when you emerge trailing streamers
of water from your skin, someone will be there,
if not at the pool's edge with a towel,
then in the darkening room to which you climb
the freckled stairs, and if not there,
then in the night that has just begun
to hum with the cicadas' cry, and, if not,
then on a day you have not yet imagined,
on which you will return to float in the pool,
arms spread out wide, your breath your buoyancy,
suspending you in an element of belief.

HUNGARIAN SONNET 1

You think that *paradicsom* is the fruit,
and fall in love again with naming. Here,
you cry, are people after my own heart,
who hang Eden and apple in one word, fat

on the tongue! But then you learn your 'paradise'
is grown on a vine, and not on a branch –
a mere tomato, *száz forint* per bunch.
You comfort yourself: the early rabbis

saw in Biblical fruit puns for desire
(citron) and destruction (carob); you note
what scholars now favor: pomegranate.
Gránátalma! It sounds to your ear

like a 'soul stone'. Ineffable, but hewn
down, somehow, still, and held tight in the hand.

LISTENING TO THE BLUES ON A THURSDAY MORNING

It's difficult to swallow,
this newfound old truth
that birdcalls loosed into a morning storm
and borne away with juniper seedlings
and flights of feather-thin seed husks
last, measured against time, as long

as any life lived to observe them.
How the bile rises in protest
at the one sure fact we have.
This is the nature of the blues:
not just being done wrong,
but not having time enough to hurt.

And so the players love the rules,
endless possibility – but
only the twelve bars to hold it.
Just a quick chance to worry
the loss between the teeth, the bits,
like the man says, goin' down slow.

RECURRENCE

Good dreams are that because they allow you
to touch the object of your desire
without the end of anticipation.
A smooth pillar of stone is cool despite
the sun that inflames the hills in the west,
and cool is the hand just before contact
with the stone, and in contact, and contact lost,
still it is cool. I dreamed not a pillar

but a smoothness all the same; not a smoothness
but a chill as of fruit on a day
of air unmoving; not a chill
but anything that could be turned to stone.
Flesh; blankets pulled up over flesh and rippled
in stillness like the folds of fabric
Bernini found beneath marble; the heart
on hearing the news. A dream of soft things

gone to hardness. This tumor, like the first ones,
was hard from the start, solid in its
invisible burgeoning. In half sleep
I dreamed my sister's desires because
I could not know them, except to know
that they had no object, only the lack —
no anticipation, no inflammation,
no sun-made heat
                    that my cold hands could cool.

TREMOR

When it started, she was still looking for her face
in the circle of water that pooled
every morning on the black granite countertop.
Somehow in the daily ritual
of coffee and toast she created always
this small puddle that stilled into the only
mirror she trusted to start her days.
It needed a moment for her features

to pull into focus; she'd mistake
the reflection of a track light for a glint
in her eye, or find a new beauty mark
in a crumb on the skim of the water.
This time, before her eyes could find her eyes
the floor pulled loose and set the puddle
running like a river to a waterfall at the edge
of the granite. She was just able, for one

second, to see what she had found of her flesh
elongate, stretched from chin to sandy hair
into little more than a thread, and vanish
at the end of the counter. She gasped,
and threw both hands forward to grasp the granite –
not to keep from falling, not in mind
of the earthquake's power to cast her
like a doll onto the floor, or to call down

a hail of plaster and pans and fixtures
freed from the ceiling into gravity,
not in the need to get to the door, not even
aware of the temblor at all, not yet: she held
herself up, shut her eyes, and opened them

so that there would be before her simply a trickle
of water, not a quicksilver looking-glass
carrying her right off the edge of the world.

AGAINST NOSTALGIA

Should've seen it coming. Drawn, as he was,
toward the smallest change in hue, he was gone
longer than even he knew in search
of the source of the blue that bled
along every bend in the river,
until, as he should have known, it was too late
to stand down and let the wash of night consume him
unremarked upon. Instead, he spoke of it

as of a memory brought by the scent
of leaves moldering or of waters stilled
into must, first in silence and to no purpose
other than to give shape to thought, but soon
aloud, and soon louder, calling the night
by name, naming the night's colors
as they blossomed with the words he might
have given her had she given him the time.

A promise in indigo, obsidian
cherished like a wish shared only once,
with more breath than voice – he should have heard
as he should have seen and he should have known
the way in which his small desolation,
once spoken, would grow out into the air
around him, as if something lost could be
anything other than a hole in the light.

ROUTE 501 SOUTH

The road is empty. On the radio
the correspondent's voice cracks with distance
from the North Pole. Each word brings insistence:
the world does stretch on, to the end, in snow.

Motion is frozen here, she says. *The waves*
have been stilled and painted white – sugared wisps
of meringue forever held before my lips.
Her figures are the only ones I have.

I think of the Pole, imagine such weather,
such blurring of day and night. Later, I will
miss this voice, like my lover, like the chills
up my spine when we wintered together.

Fogging up car windows, every breath seems
to ask why, each day, we go to extremes.

AT DINOSAUR VALLEY, GLEN ROSE, TX

Texas sugarberry in the bottoms.
Willow, cottonwood on the sandstone banks.

River waters here run brown – have done
for a million years, give or take, wearing down

to bedrock, revealing the famous footprints
kids sit in when the Paluxy runs low.

Othniel Marsh called it 'apatosaurus':
eighteen seventy-seven, a headless skeleton,

shouting *Time is not new, is not*
the purview of the small or fragile!

Marsh called his next god 'brontosaurus',
a name carried to Texas with Sinclair Oil's

fiberglass mock-up of the fearsome beast.
He was wrong, of course: deceptive lizard,

thunder lizard – two species, same genus.
Naming is no more a straight line than this

river, meandering through hills of 'oak',
'ashe juniper', and 'mesquite'. The children laugh

in the feathered sunlight, find sticks
to etch their initials – with heart-shaped frames –

in muddied patches of the exposed river bed.
And why not? Over one hundred million years'

worth of persistence in a single stone
does not guarantee that the creature

that shaped it will be recognized. Our small
scratchings in mud can hold our smiling selves —

deceptive, thunderous, impossibly large —
fast at least until the river runs high.

SURVIVAL TIP: LIVING THROUGH THE NIGHT

In the end you walked away,
out into the ribbons of smoke,
as if you were of that purple,
gray, and shifting element,
leaving me to remember
what you had said before
the first thin tendrils reached up
toward our eyes. How you gave me
what you called a lesson
in survival. In getting through.
The tinder in a flint-strike fire

is ignited by molten iron,
shaved from steel and spun
into white-hot spheres – little worlds
born of the hand's Big Bang.
The ratio, you said, is the key
to this shaping, maximizing volume,
and speed is the thing in the striking.
So strike fast, you said, not hard.
Allow stone to graze metal,
to touch it as if by accident.
Do not romanticize the softness
of the nest you have built
to hatch the flame, so perfect for fire
even had your fingers not
massaged it into readiness,
so suited to burn. That way lies night
and no warmth to fool you
into believing yourself not alone.
Strike fast. Keep the target of the sparks

at the edge of your vision.

Let the breath of the woods
be your bellows – do not give in
and face the first flicker of light,
just strike again, and fast, like a sound
barely heard at the darkened edge
of the forest, like a glance
from the eye of the falling night,
like the faintest change in the air.
Strike fast, close your eyes against small
hopes, you said,
                    and wait to feel the heat.

HOW TO TEACH THE WRITING OF POETRY

Give your student a quill pen
and an empty inkwell. Ask her
to admire the brittle tubular spine
of the feather plucked from the promise
of flight. If she is adamant
that you fill the well, use rainwater
that the words come fast and clear,
or wax that they seal themselves
as they are named. Insist, in turn,
that she laugh should the paper run to pulp,
or the wax fuse to the skin
at her fingertips. Tell her about

the coastal redwoods, how the trunks
join so that what is a tree
at its base is three trees or four
by the point at which the filtered light
first brushes the wood, and, in shadows
a third of the way up, just before
the neck begins to ache, again
is a tree. About dissonance.
About dough stretched on a floured board.
Everything that comes together
just where it comes apart. About
faith. Work. Hard words. Soft sounds. Ink stains.

#2 TRAM, BUDAPEST

No longer stiff for fear of pickpockets,
you've learned to sway, to loose your hips and join
the jelly mass of bodies. In your jeans
no map, your ears attuned, now, to the racket

of ancient metal rims that gouge the tracks
with fire, you look across the swollen river.
'The Castle' rises in a word – *Budavár* –
and you, so proud to know so small a trick

of the tongue, think 'tram' cannot do *Villamos*
the justice due to these old men whose suits
are dignified, rumpled, and ringed with soot.
It starts like this, you think: what was a mishmash

comes into focus; hands through leather straps,
you learn balance, like living, in baby steps.

THE CRICKETS & THE CEILING FAN

Summer won't stop. There is unease
behind the eyes of those few faces we see
when we walk the city streets in search
of the pink disc of the evening sun.

It reads like a suspicion
that at last the jig is up.
The equinox means nothing now.
No almanac has a name for the moon
that would predict this tying-back
of the cloud-curtain of fall.

Inside, the fan blades chase one another
past the turning of the night;
the crickets' chirp-and-whirr that once leapt
in turn from viburnum to lavender to rose
now either rises everywhere at once
or is stilled.

Somewhere the waters ride roughshod
over a barrier island. We see it
on the news: a radar image
like the palette of a painter gone mad
trying to invent the color of weather.

The crickets freed from their season
find a pitch that fits comfortably
over the voice of the announcer
tracing the swirls with a first-time
lover's awe at the elasticity
of the body. The fan blades trouble
the air, almost like wind, almost
like we are still welcome outside.

GLOBE

When I was a boy, I would spin
my grandmother's globe, just to feel
the tiny topographies, cool
like leather, under my fingers.
The Andes, the Himalayas
reduced to Braille. I would close my eyes,
and wait to see where I landed.
That was all I knew of travel.

In your eyes, I see me, but you,
you want to explore, to conquer
mountains I'd have left as fingertip
memories. You smell your own sweat
in your dreams, and know that the earth
is covered with that water.
If my finger stopped in the ocean,
I'd just spin the world one more time.

You would dive right in. Listen
to the spinning orb beneath
your fingers. That's my voice calling out
from the plastic, like music pulled
from vinyl by a tracking needle.
I'm saying, wait, it's me, I think
I'm ready, down here at the base
of a mountain you've already climbed.

THE CURVATURE OF THE EARTH

after Jules Breton's 'The Song of the Lark'

The rising sun is a blood blister
on the flattened palm of the distant farm.

The heavy billhook at the end
of the peasant girl's ramrod-straight right arm

extends from her mid-thigh, its blade
pointing down and back at her right leg,

a crescent moon poised above the fallow fields
like a warning to the dawning day:

do not linger long in this benighted landscape.
The lark, fittingly, is a mere hint

at the edge of the canvas, visible only
up close or if one knows to look for it.

It could be simply an accident of oil, a smudge
on the pea-green daybreak. Perhaps it is

a bird only in the eye of the viewer
who wants violence to have a purpose

and to come always from feeling, who sees
in the girl's faraway gaze not the same cold

tempered steel of the instrument
she holds at attention, not even a hesitancy

at facing the cutting edge of the sharpened morning,
but rather a simple obedience to the diurnal task:

turn the earth, and bring up each time a new
fleshy clod of whatever has gone before.

SNOWBOUND

With fresh memories we returned
      to the city
a step ahead of the squall.
It came in a whitewash;
we turned our attention
      to the walls.
Competition,
or, at least, imitation.
Runnels of paint drizzled along the edge
of my roller – easily smoothed
with lazy brush strokes,
as the snow fell layer upon layer
      over a city that sighed
with the weight.

I remembered
the creek packed with slush, slogging
      through powdered fields;
I plunked in snowballs for good measure.
You went ahead
      to the bridge,
snowflakes in long eyelashes
like an image in memory even
at the time.
      On the bluff the Inn smoked –
a scene from the imagined story:
wood scent, embers flitting
      over skeleton trees, or
first flakes of the coming storm.

We returned; darkness dropped
        on the city
like a shade at the frosted windows.
        At sundown, the converse:
snow in blue light
held the night at bay. We had lost time
        in the dusk all day.
The walls dried —
and sweat, and flecks of paint
        on fingernails
and rumpled, baggy clothes. I left them on,
shouldered, for form's sake, a shovel,
and stepped out in a lull
        onto the surface of the moon.

I remembered
the Inn smoked, half-hidden in pine
        on the bluff, the memory warm
like your flushed cheek
        on my shoulder. Your eyelashes brushed
my neck, swept beads of sweat
with lazy strokes. It was a story,
a movie perhaps,
or imagination only:
faded wallpaper, stone molding
        around the hearth, electric tapers at the glass,
the curve of your hip
        in the mirror just beyond the bed.

The memory fresh and you
        at rest, I watched my breath
dissipate
        under blue lights,
a city cleansed
        of motion and sound:

cars stilled, planes grounded, leaving
the scrape of my shovel and thrum
of my pulse, held close
        in my ears,
warmed under wool.

In memory rhythm
        of my heartbeat,
paint flecks on a drop cloth
were embers
        at the fireside, darkened house
gabled Inn, city pavement
country gully. Now
memory, the story, too,
snowbound.
Or could have been.
It needed only the stroke
        of your eyelashes
to brush runnels of melted snow
        along my neck
when I came back inside.

WATCHING HUMMINGBIRDS AT CEDAR CREEK LAKE, TX

A cobwebbed morning chill.
Cracked leaves drift from the ash

at the stilled water's edge,
and the first hummingbirds'

little dance begins.
A tentative darting in,

a flight back to shadowed,
spidery branches.

This continues, unbroken,
for a lazy, watched hour.

Of course, the feeder
is manmade. But, then, so

is the lake that drew us here.
So much energy spent

to keep ourselves aloft,
our efforts audible

over gentle breezes
only to those who hold

their own breaths long enough
to themselves to hear ours.

TOLL

There's nothing much to say. We try, instead,
to remember how to feel. Sometimes I think
we never should have learned to count. The dead

have better ways. They lean in, head-to-head
in blue light, teetering always on the brink,
unable quite to touch, learning instead

to share the silence. Peace. We living wed
our darkest fears to our desires, a link
we never should have made. To count the dead

is to risk the loss of the lives they led
to mathematics. To forget distinct
features. Worse, to say *This many* instead

of *No more* is cowardice. We have said
enough by now of 'how' and 'why'. We shrink.
We lie. Perhaps it's time to count the dead

promises we've piled on our pyre of dread.
To face what we have done and not to blink.
With nothing much to say, we sigh instead.
We never should have learned to count the dead.

II

et semel emissum volat
inrevocabile verbum

A word once uttered cannot be called back.

Horace, Epistles, Book 1, xviii, l. 71

WINNER

That oily puddle you're standing in,
that's the rainbow you desired
in a package you can afford.
The cracked ground between us is yours

so long as you don't cross it. The wind
that blew the papers from your hand
and over the gleaming razor wire,
that's my word of honor, my bond.

Why, the sun itself that raises up
both steam and glare from the wet concrete,
that sun I give, in consideration
of everything you've done for me,

and everything you've yet to do.
Make sure you look at it sideways,
with respect for its light, and in awe
of all the darkness it obscures.

GREATNESS

Rub the curve of the lamp as you would
a lover's shoulder after long years
of devotion. If all that escapes
is a muted, hollow sound, at least
your fingers will be well occupied.
Any act of faith is at its core a means
of busying the hands. We design
our rituals as we do our weapons:
from slingshot to longbow to trigger
to joystick, the holy work is handled
at arm's length. The feet have enough to do;
the mind has too much. There's a figure
moving slowly along a low wall, just there,
at the edge of your range. Your legs might cover
the distance your eyes have already gauged,
but not before the sweat on your palms
demands your attention and you find yourself
desperately in need of something to squeeze.

WALL

First one thing,
then the same again.
Even Snout the Tinker showed more spirit.
His was at least a human partition. It changed
from the rehearsal, where a wall was blocked anew
until it settled its weight just right,
to the stock-still held breath of its moment
at the nuptial feast, where a man was mere adornment
among forked candelabra and berry vines
curled like heat-set hair around pewter pitchers.

These days this layering is all of a piece:
a lion, a lover, even love itself, every threat
of incursion, and more slabs are laid on. Someone cries
Death himself is here, and is very long of leg,
and the architect, who never read Poe, either, it seems,
decrees that height and length alone
can forestall this approach.

It is relentless, this building, because every failure
of its logic reveals a new candidate for first enemy:
if death has shrugged a breathless sigh
and stepped aside to watch the show stretch on
into the night, then it's the dog
whose moon-cast shadow bespeaks powerful thighs,
or her mistress holding a lead
that looks made for grappling, or maybe
the breeze that carries the rattled bones of her breath
right up to the edge,
or even the dusty moon itself.

Yes, it is the very moon against which we build,
that furtive transient, always crossing and recrossing
every line we imagine onto the Earth,
never bringing quite the same light twice,
but bringing light, nonetheless, first to one side,
and, soon enough, to the other.

INDUSTRY

Oncidium volcano midnight, or 'volcano queen',
flouts a dozen five-piece blossoms in lemon, rust,
and cinnamon on every budding stalk.
Its care requires the genius only
of constancy: moderate the medium,
measure the morning sun through a gauze
of sheer curtain trimmed to filter the light,
and collect rainwater to avoid
the softening salts that tune the city's water
to our skin. Be honest about what you can
and cannot control, though this requires
that you learn to lean in and whisper nothing,
nothing, nothing. Do not promise the work.
Work the promise of every tiny shoot
that speaks of leaf or flower, knowing that none
is guaranteed to return the fiery burst
that brought you to your first devotion,
but that one might one day do so, so long
as you remain humble, unseduced
by your own glowing vision, holding up
instead the mundane dignity that bends
to the call of a workaday song.

BAN

With your hand, sketch on the air a door
at arm's length. Describe its lock
as a toy-chest keyhole sized to the space
between thumb and forefinger.
If you are in, turn the key against clouds
like smoke-tailed dogs and breezes

that might muss your hair. If out, flick your wrist
and open a portal to a silent room
furnished just for you in the ivory, silk,
and marble of your dearest dream. The one
where no laugh passes a lip you have not
bruised. You cannot help a nibble here,

a reflex there, sending you back across
the transom of your brutal youth. Beauty
marked you alone, you felt. You knew the taste
you'd leave in beauty's mouth ever after
if once you learned to teach her the distance
from her measured breath to your shaking hand.

FORCE

At a rickety folding card table
topped with stretched plastic in a wood-grain print
sits the fortune teller you have hired
to entertain the notion of your own
endurance. She licks the pink fingertips
of one hand to wet a single spit curl
to the powder-bright forehead below
her paisley head scarf. With the other
she holds your wrist to the table, just as you
have taught her to do. This obedience

quickens your pulse the same way a child's
soundless first tears do in the moment
before the cries begin, as the blood
starts to flow. You know the script
you've written to a word, and the feathered lashes,
silver-moon earrings, and red-as-sin lipstick
of the costume you have designed are enough
to keep you from hearing the ironic laugh
behind the voice telling you how long
she has waited to hold your heart in her hands.

DEAL

Pitch me. Let the current of your offer
hum along my spine. Tickle my bones
with the blood-rush that comes with the first
glimpse of the auction block. Sell me

on the promise of a mighty return
on every dollar I nail to the arm
of your golden high-backed chair. I'll buy
my own self

              if you price it just right.

CARNAGE

Lawn mowers and edge trimmers scatter
the bodies with abandon. Guard dogs
show their teeth to the invisible fences.

Overnight, an incursion of ADT signs
colonizes the neighborhood, and takes
no prisoners. The killers come to call

weep to feel so welcome. Even the trees
back-lit by a rising moon crackle
in the breeze like the pulsating sounds

of the Tasers whose light show we all know
from TV. Imagine our horror,
having to brave the naked cul-de-sacs

where glacial erratics stand sentinel
in every yard, heavy reminders
of the burdens of this modern life,

while down every street run rivers of blood
coaxed from these stones no one knew to be
so sanguine on the topic of human pain.

WORK

Rain on the skylight like fingertips
drumming on the lid of boredom.
Knowing it's in there, it's hard not to want
to let it out, to see if it's really worse
than the task at hand. When you're a cog
in the machinery of someone else's dream,
you obey the laws of physics
and turn until friction forbids it.

The neon tubes of the dream marquee hiss
and sputter unseen out front. The dreamer
sleeps and conjures variations on a theme:
bodies aglow in a tar-dark room,
moving with one will in concentric rings
around the altar whose sacrifice
is bored indeed of the role, ready now
to awaken and find that the job is done.

SECURITY

... blankets the whole of the yard
in a latticework of lines we can't see.
The sensors can. Their eyes are spider-scoped
and rodent-tuned. The lights they trigger
are like synapses in the mind
of the state, firing along a sequenced path
of their own making, bleaching in turn
every tuft of growth, to show
that nothing can abide there long
unseen. To a viewer from without
the chain-link horizon, it must be
as a proscenium stage managed
by an old man with a mania
for the quick reveal and the sudden
blackout. You suspect he would have
a smile he kept always to himself,
for fear that its teeth would tear a hole
in his particular patch of darkness
just big enough to show you a flash
of what he would rather not be made of.

REFUGE

Where we bury the body. The light
reveals nothing but darkness, and peace
is a stone cross damp with condensation,
cool like the shade that erases the words
we don't need to see anyway. *Could love
have kept her, she would still be here.* Be still.

Voices gather, and fall away, somewhere
close at hand. Memory is a silenced footfall.
We cannot measure its approach in time,
relying instead on the tickle
at the nape of the neck, knowing that this touch
will not be withheld for long in the end.

THREAT

Everyone agrees: we are enduring
a bitter season, cold-shouldering
past one another as if our tracks
once laid at our heels will abide
and show themselves straight
should we lose our way in the dark of day.
Danger lies only in hesitation. To be sure
is to be true. A canny proposition,
this consensus that everyone
is equally aggrieved by every storm.

It implicates even the crocuses,
just here in the mud-and-mulch bed
in the lee of the house. Their truth, too,
must be relative, no more valid
than some unflowering at work
in another small yard, some not-poking-through
in an annual act of defiance,
an anti-coloring of dark, wet earth
with pastel wisps of dawn. The non-bulbs
that dis-announce the coming of spring
were not plopped, with dirt and a little hope,
by gardeners never down on their knees,
in holes just big enough to cradle the hearts
of all those things that would reach for the light.

III

SAN ANTONIO TRIPTYCH

I
THE DEVIL'S BALLROOM

Don Albert's ghost leads a ghoulish swing band
through its paces even today. He died
in San Antone in 1980. But hide
your eyes from the ruins of The Shadowland,

and tune your ears to the baked-clay jazz
of the territory band whose brass charts
so gladdened the feet and lightened the heart,
and you'll hear the tunes drifting through the gauze

of the years. Albert blew with Troy Floyd's boys
from 'twenty-six to 'twenty-nine, then led
a band whose every brazen horn swell said,
We bring you sin and all its host of joys.

The Ballroom grew so hot with Albert's sound
that the whole damned place burned straight to the ground.

II
RICHARD WIDMARK DEFENDS THE ALAMO

The Duke was the main attraction, of course.
My aunt would mimic that slung-from-the-hip
walk if you dared to give her any lip,
and for a little boy a show of force

is filmic, brave, and unironic. Guns
are tongues that talk the bully to his knees.
But something in my childish fantasies
feared and therefore preferred the one-on-one

intimacy of the blade. Jim Bowie,
a Tennessee import baptized in Texas,
held my gaze to the screen. Much as sex is
to adolescence, blood lust is to he

who would be a hero in tube-blue light.
I felt myself raw, just spoiling for a fight.

III
'HIJOS DALGOS'

A bastardization of *the children*
of something, which in this case truly was
something, since *algo* connoted riches
unknown to all but the most fearsome men.

The King imagined two hundred island
families trading the old colony
for the new. It made sense: the Canaries
invited war with wealth; you'd understand

that death comes to the master and to the slave,
having been the one and lashed the other,
if you came from Tenerife. Another
land: one more conjugation of *to have*.

Besides: the acequias carried water
pure as the blood of any native daughter.

AGAINST DESPAIR

He met her in a wish for colder weather.
He took the sweat of long days,
an Indian Summer that wouldn't end,
and brought it with him to an oak table,
streaked with grease, by a corner window,
and there she was.

She brought to him tea steeping in a glass
demitasse and from him a vow to learn
everything, beginning with patience.
It was, at least, a daily way to pass
for human, and the time as well.
He used his mother's mantra:

to be a better listener, ask better questions.
Before her last name, her favorite lunar phase;
before the town where she was happy,
the color of the eyes of her first
lost childhood pet. She smiled each word
with a glance at the ceiling:

waxing gibbous, Gibson, island blue
and Blue Island. Her answers fell around him
like leaves of snow, each one alone
its distinct self, their accumulation
a testament to what can pass with the breath
of a new wind, bringing a change in the season.

LETTING DOWN YOUR GUARD

Flattened by the fall, you have time to ponder
physics and the dust mote that catches your eye
as it crosses a shaft of pearled light
before you get back up. It flashes itself
into consequence for just the one second
needed to put you in mind of a house fire
you saw years ago. Everyone you knew
gathered around and held a distance

born more of awe than of the need to pay heed
to instructions crackling into the night
in a filtered tin voice broadcast
through an invisible loudspeaker. The voice
spoke of danger – you knew that even though
you did not hear the words exactly,
and were not interested in the warnings
of adults. You already knew much

about risk, standing there in your bare legs,
knobby knees below hand-me-down shorts
one size too big held tight in your hands.
You crouched to stare at the blaze reflected
in a puddle of water that had leaked
from the fire engine whose nasal siren song
had called you out past your mother's wishes.
Embers and sparks danced across the whole

of the tiny lake like miraculous insects
born at one shore and extinguished by the other.
Having found this perfect and still window
into loss, you were hard-pressed to look back
to the main event as it unfolded

in others' lives lived so nearby and so
very far away. And this, you think now,
waiting for another fleck of dust

to burst into life in the filtered wash
of the mid afternoon, is what you have done
again that has brought you to the edge
from which you have allowed yourself to fall:
tuned out repeated warnings that amplified
a caution you'd already felt, and given
yourself to the study of miracles –
those things that cannot be, but, simply, are.

PATH OF TOTALITY

Muzzle flash. Envy's flush.
Fission fire. White fear.
Crescent sun. Unfiltered sin.

So many things not to be
looked at head-on.
To face them is to risk
being changed, the after-glow
of what you've seen
a scar in the mirror.

Why take the chance, anyway?
You know what's there
between your head and the divine.
Keep your eyes on the shadows
the leaves draw in the dirt.

If there's a darkness
coming down, no need to lift
your gaze to meet it. Pretend
it's the voice from the angel
shoulder you hear, whispering,
Whatever you do, my child,
however much you know
that this is not a masking
but a revealing, however
needful the call to level
your chin to the horizon
and then not to stop there,
do us both a favor —

do not look up.

FROM A MCDONNELL-DOUGLAS MD 80

Clouds like field ice on the surface
of the sky below us. Where the cloud ice
parts, miraculous pools reveal
the sea-bed earth, geometries
in greens and browns, demarcating
the still boundless industry
of people so much unlike
the just-hatched fish they might resemble
from a height, though from up here
we would not see them at all.
Where the clouds take on more
the colors and shapes of sands after wind,
a dunescape flecked with quartz pink
and gold. Where the cloud fields end,
a shelf on which might sit a goddess
in repose, silver legs dangling,
untouchable toes with nails painted
every color men cannot see
reaching down just to the tops
of the tallest buildings, fanning
out across the mortal realms
a scent that, even if the air
were water, would still change the name
of the night, falling more slowly
on you, in the west, than on me,
at thirty thousand feet and holding
steady, wanting not to land
and needing, all the same, to come down.

A LULLABY IN MARCH

The wildest winds of the season sing
more than threaten if you listen just right:

if you stand still enough that your spine
begins to feel like some new part of you,

if you still your breath and tune to the one
that whips out of the Northwest and down

through your street, you can hear the voices raised
in harmony miles and miles again

from the church of your first believing.
How you willed the damp like midnight dew

away, blinking it back, drying your bones
as from the inside out you taught yourself

to stand, like the skeleton trees at the edge
of the graveyard, aligned with the day

but outside the weather. The tune might be
one you hummed once, one your sister taught you

to settle the ghosts you both knew grew
restless at just this time of the year:

a song of the bereaved, offered to
the spirits that they not linger long bereft.

PLANETARIUM

In your city, constellations
come and go not with clouds,
but with industry, the hard labor
of a people trying to make the stars
redundant. My small town has its share
of open sky, though it would be easy
to say that the brightest stars
come and go with your visits.

You would live without a ceiling,
city or no, and shine your own light
back at whatever fell in
from above. You see stars where most
see ash. Easy to say, that I would
pull the constellations in for you
and cast them like splatters of paint
on the barren walls of your room.

But what is not easy to say
is that as I let you conjure
the heavens, and banish the plaster
from above us, whole galaxies
disappear with each turning
of your head. If you must step away
even for a moment, please turn
the stars back on before you go.

BLACK MOON

The third new moon of four in one season.
We call the equivalent full moon blue.
But we never say, *Once in a black moon,*
now do we? That sounds wrong, for some reason.

It's cool to feel blue – like you're candle-lit
through stained glass, holy in your longing, loss,
or love. But to feel black? Pedro said, *Boss,*
there's one thing we don't do, and that is it.

Puerto Rican, not black, he called everyone
on the loading dock who wasn't in charge
Boss, and knew whereof he spoke. He grew large
with wisdom, and said, *Color is a gun*

we point at our inadequacies. True.
But truth won't make a black moon of the blue.

MORE FLIES WITH HONEY

Like strawberries or the ripest of pears,
her sweetness was tart at the edges and just

a bit too much. This was her mother's
endless refrain, and had it been about any

product of her hands, any item on which
she worked other than herself, she would not

have minded much. As it was, she sighed
in silence and took it all too closely to her heart.

Mother, she said, *come sit on the porch.*
Rattan chairs with striped foam pads, purchased

for the comfort of the one person
who always removed hers before sitting.

*This is how it is: I will laugh like the child
I no longer am, like a kicked tin can*

*clattering, then spinning to rest, and cry
when you'd rather I not.* She made no more

of it, and leaned toward the swing, on whose slats
she laid the discarded pad. Her mother's smile

was like a gleaming candy wrapper tied
and turned up neatly at both ends. To love,

she thought, as to be loved, is to measure
the distance of a breath, and to hold it.

TUTORIAL

Marriage is the key to murder,
she says. Meaning, loving someone
long enough to want love to be
a memory, a story told
over a rusty hour in the dark
so as to justify the blade
sharpened on a stone meant only
for decoration.
                She knew me
first in my role as storyteller,
the funny man with everything
but the jangle-bell cap and gold felt shoes
to mark him out as a joker:
to wit, I once made her laugh.
But what she says now is no more
accusation than proposal.
She wants merely
                to test the waters
of my wishes, to fathom
the depth of my desire. To see
if I am ready to tell the truth.
But who would wish to hear of nights
through which I lie down as if alone,
a killing frost just beyond the glass,
a stillness by my side stretching out
its neck to fill

                my open, empty hands?

PRAYING MANTIS

Exaggerated to cartoonish proportions,
the silhouette outside the thin cotton curtains
waited all sun long as we lay in an old twin bed
in a slanted attic room just above the breeze:
a praying mantis, unmistakable
in its mock supplication, still and solemn
before the shadows of leaves just beyond
the screen, dancing lightly, like fingers on skin.

The flowered sheets were starched with sweat
we had spent so easily, under wet breath
and wild flashes of iris in pink candlelight.
If the mantis had arrived in the night,
we had missed it, despite ample moonlight
and the drifting time spent facing the window,
gazing out over the curves of our bodies,
rising and falling with every shared breath.

But our visitor probably arrived
at sun-up, with the wash of birdsong
and muted traffic in the neighborhood below.
And as it perched, observing the Sabbath,
so too did we linger, not moving
as the light changed behind it and we faded
in and out like static, crackling softly
over a low, forgotten frequency.

When the new dusk came, the mantis was gone.
The leaf shadows were purple; the curtains began
to push in with a shift in the wind. When we noticed
the empty spot on the screen, you looked at me
as if to say, you got away with it this time.

We had done nothing all day. I smiled.
Your look said, today the blood still runs in your veins.
You smiled. Maybe next time, I will bleed you dry.

TO THE BOY SITTING IN A LONDON LEAF-FALL, HIS BACK AGAINST A WET ALDER TREE

You coax us out of thought and into memory, the curves
of your shoulders, which will not ache when you unfurl them
once this mood has passed, the shapes of the paths back to our own
adolescent discontentments.

This is not to patronize:
we dare not dishonor your isolation, the way a tongue
of your rain-heavy hair licks against your brow, dripping
onto your lashes a moisture you would not allow there
otherwise, because it was ours.

Is ours, in those moments
when, together or apart, we remember that we are apart always,
knowing the ridges at the backs only of our own teeth,
the familiar murmurings, in sudden silences,
only of our own ears.

No, we know to praise you,
to wish we could stop to raise you into the cool day,
our fingers hooked under the arms of your baggy sweatshirt,
the borrowed gravity of your temporary sorrow
giving purpose to the hands

we have been surprised, lately,
to find still hanging at the ends of arms we do not wrap
around each other as we should, with the same desperate need
that has wrapped yours around your chest, your eyes open
into the space in front of you,

your back scratched at its base
by the bark of your tree – the posture of youth knowing
what those who've survived it forget, that one danger in living
lies in uncurling ourselves into the world every day,
the risk of exposure exceeded

only by the risk
of forgetting how to be exposed, how to put our backs
into it, how to blink away the rain and stare wide-eyed
into the certainty of more uncertain weather.

MILE STONES

Lichen and moss define
centuries-old characters
like a tombstone rubbing
in green-gray pencil:
seventeen miles to Falmouth.

Over the next hill
the road bends
into sycamore and beech;
a fine mist gathers
on the leaves; the smell
is the dank end
of an autumn day.

> *She had green eyes, like lake water*
> *shot through with sharp light*
> *at mid-afternoon. Sometimes,*
> *it was as if I could touch her*
> *just by thinking soft thoughts.*

I walk for an hour beyond
the seventeen-mile stone,
to the next ancient marker easing
through the undergrowth:
seventeen miles to Falmouth.

One more hill, another bend
in the road, tomorrow's mist —
she is etched in memory,
and there are no figures
carved in stronger stone
to help me measure
how far I have come.

PUPPY LOVE

for Ruthie and Phillip

What lasts? Often those things we're told
will not: the sting of a cut on the knee
when we've run too fast down the cracked sidewalks
of childhood, chalked yellow, pink, and blue
with crooked stars and faces like letters
in alphabets we've invented to tell
stories the big kids will not understand;

the last blush of evening light at the point
where the river meets the sky and seems
to run from dusk back into the day, ferrying
ribbons of gold upstream to where, unbelieving,
we watch from the banks the currency
of time returning, if only to our eyes;
the ache like a weight that pulls the shoulders down

at a hand withdrawn without warning;
the sound of a note pedaled by the stillness
around it, not by its player; the preening burst
of a lily cut with an imperfect blade
and fed only on a wish for beauty
and a little water in an old milk bottle;
and, at last, a love that falls into us

more than we into it — a love like
weather, changing even the cast of the sky,
of the shadows that merge where our heads are bowed,
changing the ways we play out games begun
when we were kids, dancing into our lives
as into the rain that ends the drought
that started when we weren't looking and lasted

until we noticed, a love like language,
a way of saying that we're here, that we will
be here, a love like breathing –

$\qquad\qquad\qquad\qquad$ a love like yours.

UNTOUCHED

No cats in the garden, no cats holding court,
suffering the sparrows that gather
at the trellises, harden in the light,
and still the gaze before moving on. Bold
in the night of shadow and pitch, degrees

of not-light, they are gone this purpled dawn.
I should be glad of the peace. Of the soft peace
that might be grace if I believed what you said,
stretching, with that feline yawn. *I am so glad.*
How relieved you were to know me untroubled,

to see me from afar, as through a lens
held out at arm's length. We measure distance
just so: star to eye, memory to blood.
I miss your body not known to me, sins
not tasted, a good story not to tell.

THE NEXT DAY

The will constricts. *To do* becomes *have done*.
Of all the amber stains the dappled light
of morning spreads across the body, none
reveals the wound that matters. None has quite

the look or feel of scattered shot, how holes
converge and bleed as one. How presence drains
the past of love. How memory extolls
the pain as virtue undersold, a grain

of poison pressed beneath the tongue
until its burn subsides. It's not enough
to splinter the sun, the jagged shards hung
like teeth from a string at the throat, to toughen

up, to shut it down. There's still the matter
of what remains. The chalk outline. The splatter.

IN PRAISE OF MORTALITY

Lords over fragile things, but not fragile
themselves, the gods have rarely suffered beauty
gladly. A stone freed from its mountainside
mooring that falls into the gorse, and fans

the flattened fronds out, creating a cavity
much like that space in the chest where the heart
of the passerby, so nearly crushed,
begins again to beat – this does not impress.

What can a heartbeat mean to the gods,
who made the engine of the blood a clockwork toy,
wound it up, turned it loose, and soon
lost interest? The briefly-treasured doll

thus driven may be crushed by the stone, may
not. She may catch her breath to behold
the sliver of tangerine sun, vanishing
in clouds behind the peak of the stone's fall.

Or she may not. She may not see the sun
or, seeing it, she may give her breath instead
to a sigh at the thought of the sounds
she'd have missed, just a step to the right:

the cry of an ember snapped from a pine log,
the whistle-smooth *ess* of the voice of a man
she has met only once and now misses.
She has a breath to give, and this is all.

All she needs to outstrip the graceful gods
in grace are the heart almost stopped
and the lungs nearly stilled. What do the gods know
of gratitude, the sting of the sweat's salt

in the eye of she who beholds her own going on,
who knows that one day the stone will not miss,
who knows that she will breathe and not, unlike
the gods, without body or breath to bleed?

IV

VAVILOV AT SARATOV

From late 1941 until January 1943,
Nikolay Ivanovich Vavilov was held in one
of Stalin's gulag prisons, in Saratov, Russia. Vavilov
was the greatest agricultural botanist in the Soviet
Union, and perhaps in the world. He had developed
theories about crop diversity that still dominate the field
today, and had curated the 'seed vault' that became the
model for all such subsequent collections dedicated to
preserving the history and the future of the human race's
agricultural endeavors. Vavilov had fallen more and more
out of favor with Stalin over the years, his place usurped
by Trofim Lysenko, a rival botanist whose theories about
plant heredity were attractive to the science-skeptical
Party leadership, though Vavilov
knew them to be fraudulent.

I
WINTER 1942-43: A PRISON YARD IN AN OUTPOST OF STALIN'S GULAG; SARATOV, RUSSIA

The irony of a growing hunger could not
have been lost on the man who would feed the world,
but even irony bows to hallucination.
What did he see there, pacing away the spit-grey
mornings behind the wire? Perhaps what we all see
in half-light: shadings of desire. The past
a catalogue of seductions, a seed bank
of every wish that did or did not flower

but that had in it the latent power
to do so. His body imprisoned finally
in the town where he'd made his reputation
years before, Vavilov's feverish thoughts
must have danced in and out of time, to light
again and again on the petal-soft edges
of the one longing whose genetic structure
would be passed down to all those that followed.

II
AUGUST 1940: ON A HILLSIDE IN THE
CARPATHIAN MOUNTAINS; UKRAINE

Not the longing simply to be left alone,
which must have taken him that sun-baked day
in the burgeoning fields of mountain wheat
that lay along the track of his last solo hike,
as it can take any of us when we suspect
that we are more depended-upon than
dependable. Did he see the black sedan
roll back down the mountain road to wait?

It would have looked like a drop of soiled water
sliding off a leaf. Or did he hear the cough
of the engine, or did he simply know
that this was the day they must come for him,
this day of one last triumphant find, his rucksack
heavy with grain hardy enough to withstand
the abuses that nature dispenses so
dispassionately, so unlike the blows of men?

III
LATE 1941: THE PRISON YARD AT SARATOV

Not the longing merely to be of use
again, which is what he promised his jailers
he would be once he'd been moved to Saratov.
Look, he must have said, *every day I rise
to my full height, doff this shabby cap, and unfurl
the wonders even of these sparse grasses, clumped
at the base of the cracked, creaking barracks wall.*
He did so, and was reportedly well-received.

What must he have wanted to say (though too dutiful
to say it) to that rabble of scientists out
of favor? *We have sown in the jagged
furrows of our minds the seedlings of ideas
that could save the world! Close your eyes and see
what I see, sprouts growing up from Comrade Stalin's
skin, filling his mouth, snaking through his nostrils
to take up residence behind those still black eyes!*

IV
1936: THE OFFICE OF VYACHESLAV
MIKHAILOVICH MOLOTOV, STALIN'S
RIGHT-HAND-MAN; MOSCOW

Not the childish, almost irresistible longing
to jump up on Comrade Molotov's desk,
hang his arms akimbo in the posture
of a marionette, and perform a jig
punctuated by a hey here and a ha there
and one swift kick to that round, ever-smiling
face, cracking the nose-piece of the glasses
with the nose, then another, firmly planting

his heavy boot in the mouth below that parody
of Stalin's mustache. *Oh, to make the Party
taste the soil together with the spit and blood
it so fetishizes. Oh to force down the throat
the teeth so often bared and render toothless
the shit-eating grin of the State.* Instead,
he said something like, *Comrade, can we not work
together to reap what Mother Russia has sown?*

V
MARCH 1939: MEETING OF THE ALL-UNION
INSTITUTE OF PLANT BREEDING; LENINGRAD

Not that rarest of longings, the one utterly
fulfilled, as when Vavilov donned one more time
the natty three-piece suit and just-so fedora
and told the All-Union meeting once and for all
what he thought of Lysenko's pseudo-science.
The fool believes that if a stalk of wheat
bends to the East in the winds of the steppe,
this bowing will be encoded in its seed –

that a corn stalk sunburned to rust will bear
generations so stained from the root, is what
he did not say. Nor, *Millions will die, their bellies*
ballooned into famine's cruel parody
of bodies over-fed, because this man
dare not admit that he is wrong. Rather:
We shall go to the fire, we shall burn, but
we shall not retreat from our convictions.

VI
1932-33: THE LAST EXPEDITION ABROAD;
CENTRAL AND SOUTH AMERICA

Not the longing to complete a masterwork
that, wedded to a long-indulged wanderlust,
drove him to visit fourteen countries right when
the twin veils of famine and political disaster
were being drawn down on Russia. The rainforest
vibrated with life; forty-five-year-old legs
still thrilled to the ache after the day's hike.
And Vavilov had certainly read his Keats:

to glean this teeming brain meant to unearth
the secrets of every highland farmstead,
of every canopied crop-cradle of jungle.
He slept only when there was no earth at hand
to scour, as when the little plane jerked up
and down on the puppet strings of a storm,
and those still in favor with the Party screamed
in a terror Vavilov had long since blinked away.

VII
1920-21: PETROGRAD (LATER LENINGRAD)

Not the longing we all think of first, expressed
in terms like those of his letter of November 5
to Yelena Barulina, his Lenochka,
second lover and first love: *I am quite ready*
to give my life for the smallest things... She
surely did not expect that sentence to end
with *like the way your fingers curl into your palms*
when you sleep, or the faded mark like a seed husk

under the hair at the nape of your neck,
or the impression of warmth your body
would bring to this dusk-colored room in a cold,
empty city. How desperately he wanted her
to join the team that would collect, catalogue,
and conserve the means of reproduction.
The one desire wrapped around the other.
Of course his sentence ended *in science.*

VIII
JUNE 1920: THE UNIVERSITY AT SARATOV AND THE MICHURIN ORCHARDS

Not the dream that the wizard of Kozlov
would have somewhere on his unruly little farm
one of the missing links Vavilov sought,
a longing embraced by those who now dubbed him
'Biology's Mendeleev'. The visions
he must have had as waves of applause lifted
his chin ever higher, of a peach pit
poking through sticky-soft flesh, or a cutting

from an apple tree that would slowly grow
to fill a space between species in the great ledger
of cultivated life. If his imaginings
included the man as well, Vavilov would soon find
that Michurin in fact had the sorcerer's beard,
and a limb-heavy frame perfect for a tree man.
The air held the scented-soap taste of apricots.
Every seed pod handed down cast its spell.

IX
1906-1910: THE PETROVSKAYA AGRICULTURAL ACADEMY; MOSCOW

Not the charcoal sketch of a future self
that some of us plan to trace in ink
and others to rub out before anyone
can see the contours of our limitations.
Vavilov's letters from the Petrovka
folded themselves over with doubt. A good sign
for the future success of the book-burdened boy
in love more with the world than with himself.

Those green years saw the germination
of a self-assurance that he could trust.
Where the confidence man thinks, *If I make large
the tin horn of my voice and the gestures of small
hands, I can bend the soft spine of the world,*
a confident one simply gets on with the job.
Vavilov displayed a facility for words
in languages both spoken and embodied.

X
1912: THE BOTANICAL INSTITUTE AT CAMBRIDGE

Not the conviction that if only he could
squint at the marginalia scrawled in Darwin's
cramped script until the buttercream leather scent
soured to a mildew-tinged tang, then all
of what the master had not known would appear
before Vavilov's eyes like words scribbled
on a slate board by an unseen hand. A longing
for the body to be the mind, and the mind

a portal ever-opening. Newly wed
into a marriage of minds, he did Katya
a disservice, no doubt, and perhaps she did him
one as well. Unafraid now to aspire
to be what his forebear called a millionaire
of facts, he collected. His equal or better
with questions and answers, Yekaterina
planned to study, and not to be studied.

XI
1916: THE PAMIR HIGHLANDS OF BUKHARA AND
AFGHANISTAN, ALONG THE RIVER PYANDZH

Not what the glacial melt whispered to him
as it ran to egg-white pools among fields
of ancient wheat and rye where the vistas
took away whatever breath the altitude
did not: that he had been right in guessing
that the greatest centers of crop diversity
lay not along the lowland banks of the Tigris,
but at the feet of the clouds. A longing

to continue the ascent despite every
almost-disaster — the horse that bolted
on a mountain track barely a horse wide,
the churning waters that must be crossed though they
bear away both beast and burden, the cold shoulder
of the glacier slowing the blood and draining
the will in the night. For here were crops unseen
by anyone who did not subsist upon them.

XII
1917-19: THE UNIVERSITY AT SARATOV

Not even the longing that gives us the word,
that stretched distance between the first flutter
in the pulse and any chance at a sign
that someone else might have felt it. The space
between Lenochka's pale eyes lent power
to her gaze. Only the always-cocked left brow
suggesting tolerant indulgence kept it
from being too much for him to love her.

As soldiers of the Revolution crossed
and re-crossed the university's farm,
the plant man led his students to far-flung fields
where new growth might remain undisturbed. Lenochka
understood before he did. Upheaval
was the order of the day. Long before
Vavilov was imprisoned in Saratov,
he was, in that self-same city, set free.

XIII
1890S: NEAR THE MOSCOW SUBURB OF
PRESNYA

But, in the end, the longing he could not name
the first time he felt it, gigging for frogs
among rain-softened reeds in the swirled-mud
shallows of the Presnya River, or digging deep,
careful to preserve the root mass of every plant
he collected on Gusev Island. A child
of six or seven embodies that purest
of desires: the need, at last, just to know.

To know if and how the winter-chilled blood
still moves during hibernation. To learn
where in a single seed that is no larger
than a lost tooth resides the plant or tree.
To understand how a world whose sheer size
Nikolai was just beginning to sense
could grow at once immeasurable bounty
and famine. Some things once known can be changed.

XIV
JANUARY 26, 1943: THE PRISON AT SARATOV

And some cannot. Vavilov must have heard
something of the siege of Leningrad;
though it began more than a year after
he was plucked off that mountainside to rot
at the pleasure of the Party, and though
he could only imagine his protégés
at the Institute, fingers dyed blue with cold,
fending off their countrymen and rats alike,

he knew he had trained them well to protect
at peril of their own lives the currency
that might one day purchase security
for millions not yet begun. That some would slip
away, starved to death in rooms rich with grain
enough to sustain them through the war's end,
would not have surprised him had he known it.
Was he not prepared himself to do the same?

Vavilov's vision wavered. The prison yard yawned.
Katya and Lenochka took their turns naming
the colors he had seen in the fields, planting
in his last hours promises for whatever
was to come. The vault of memory itself
would not be moved any more than the vast store
of what he'd learned could be hidden from the future.
He died wanting, but not needing, to know more.

NOTES

I

Hungarian Sonnet 1
Hungarian words: 'paradicsom' = tomato; 'száz forint'
= one hundred forints, or about fifty American cents or
forty British pence; 'gránátalma' = pomegranate.

#2 Tram, Budapest
'Budavár' in this context refers specifically to the 'Buda
Castle', a fortified palace in the Buda hills of Budapest,
overlooking the Danube River; today the Castle
building houses the Hungarian National Gallery and the
Budapest History Museum. 'Villamos' is the collective
name of a particular set of street-level trams in Budapest.

The Curvature of the Earth
Breton's 'The Song of the Lark' is part of the permanent
collection of the Art Institute of Chicago.

III

San Antonio Triptych
I The Devil's Ballroom
Don Albert, who is believed to have been the first
bandleader to use the term 'swing' in advertising
his group, was once in residence at San Antonio's
Shadowland Ballroom as a horn player, and later led his
own band there and elsewhere in the city.

II Richard Widmark Defends the Alamo
In the 1960 film *The Alamo*, produced by and starring

John Wayne, Wayne played Davy Crockett; Richard Widmark portrayed Jim Bowie.

III 'Hijos Dalgos'
In the 1720s, the King of Spain promised titles to Canary-Island colonists willing to settle the first secular outpost at San Antonio.

IV

Vavilov at Saratov
For further reading on Nikolai Vavilov's remarkable life and work, please see Peter Pringle's *The Murder of Nikolai Vavilov* (Simon & Schuster, New York, 2008), Gary Paul Nabhan's *Where Our Food Comes From: Retracing Nikolai Vavilov's Quest to End Famine* (Island Press, Washington, D.C., 2009), and Scott Chaskey's *Seedtime: On the History, Husbandry, Politics, and Promise of Seeds* (Rodale Books, New York, 2014).

ACKNOWLEDGEMENTS

Grateful acknowledgement is made to the following publications, in which some of these poems first appeared, sometimes in different forms:

Anthology: 'Praying Mantis'
Bacopa Literary Journal: 'Against Despair'
Barrow Street: 'Listening to the Blues on a Thursday
      Morning'
Chautauqua: 'How to Teach the Writing of Poetry'
DMQ Review: 'The Curvature of the Earth'
Emrys Journal: 'At Dinosaur Valley'
Evansville Review: 'Tremor'
The Fourth River: 'Survival Tip: Living through
      the Night'
Kindred: 'A Lullaby in March'
Pacific Coast Journal: 'Planetarium'
Plainsongs: 'Globe'
Potomac Review: 'Watching Hummingbirds at Cedar
      Creek Lake, TX'
riverSedge: 'Industry'
Sequestrum: 'Ban'; 'Threat'; 'Winner'
So To Speak: 'More Flies with Honey'
South Dakota Review: 'Mile Stones'
Southwest Review: 'Hungarian Sonnet 1'
Unsplendid: '#2 Tram, Budapest'
Western Humanities Review: 'Recurrence'
The Worcester Review: 'Snowbound'

'Route 501 South' first appeared in the Gival Press anthology *Poetic Voices Without Borders*, as winner of the Gival Press Tri-Language Poetry Contest.

'San Antonio Triptych III: "Hijos Dalgos"' first
appeared as an art installation in the San Antonio
Cultural Commons, as part of Gemini Ink's celebration
of the city's 300th anniversary, *Thirty Poems for the
Tricentennial: A Poetic Legacy*. Many thanks to artist/
designer Coral Diaz.

Some of these poems appeared (sometimes in different
forms) in the Anchor & Plume Press chapbook *A Hole in
the Light*.

Thanks are due to countless teachers and mentors
without whose guidance, support, and wisdom this book
would never have been possible. They are far too many
to name here without my accidentally omitting a few.
For a start, I owe a deep debt to the writers and teachers
of: School District 97 in Oak Park, IL; Oak Park and
River Forest High School; Carleton College; Temple
University; the Napa Valley Writers' Conference; The
Sewanee Writers' Conference; and the Poetry at Round
Top Festival.

Willard Spiegelman has been an inspiration and an
invaluable guide to the world of poetry for twenty
years. Jim Kates, with whom I was paired in AWP's
'writer-to-writer' program in 2017, has done more than
any other individual to help to shepherd this collection
into its current form.

My students and faculty peers have always pushed me
not just as a teacher, but as a writer and as a person.
Thank you to the thousands of young writers and
the hundreds of fellow teachers with whom I have

worked, and alongside whom I have learned, at: The
Johns Hopkins University's Center for Talented Youth
summer programs; Lancaster Country Day School (PA);
St. Stephen's and St. Agnes School (VA); César Chávez
Public Charter School for Public Policy (DC); Teleki
Blanka Gimnasium (Budapest, Hungary); Trinity Valley
School (TX); and La Jolla Country Day School (CA).
Some among you have continued to work with me, on
your own writing and on mine, for many years; I hope
to have the chance to inscribe an individual note of
thanks to each of you in the near future.

Thanks to Michael Anania, Jenny Molberg, and Tomás
Morín, each of whom has been an inspiration; your
generous words mean a great deal.

Thank you to Todd Swift, John Penny, Alex Wylie,
Edwin Smet and the whole team at Eyewear Publishing
not just for believing in this collection, but for all of
your dedicated and thoughtful work in bringing it into
the world.

My family has been unfailingly supportive since I wrote
my first 'books' on stapled-together sheets of typewriter
paper in the late 1970s. Every piece I've ever published
has existed only because of such lifelong love and care.

Finally, Madison, you have believed in this book since
the first time I mentioned it as a goal toward which I
hoped to work. I simply could not have turned that
initial hazy vision into reality without you.